Elegant Mandala Coloring

Copyright: Published in the United States by Scott McDowell
Published January 2017
ISBN-13: 978-1542651394
ISBN-10: 1542651395

Thank you

www.ingramcontent.com/pod-product-compliance
Lightning Source LLC
Chambersburg PA
CBHW081554280526
45788CB00011B/3474

* 9 7 8 1 5 4 2 6 5 1 3 9 4 *